英韵李杜美诗②

A Poetry Anthology of Du Fu

by **Du Fu** [Tang Dynasty]
translated by **Xia Han**

杜甫美诗（汉英对照）

（唐）杜 甫◎著

夏 晗◎编 / 译

九 州 出 版 社
JIUZHOUPRESS

图书在版编目（CIP）数据

英韵李杜美诗．2，杜甫美诗 ：汉英对照 /（唐）杜甫著 ；夏晗编、译．-- 北京 ：九州出版社，2023.9
ISBN 978-7-5225-2111-4

Ⅰ．①英… Ⅱ．①杜… ②夏… Ⅲ．①英语－汉语－对照读物②杜诗－诗集 Ⅳ．① H319.4：I

中国国家版本馆 CIP 数据核字（2023）第 163814 号

目 录

CONTENTS

杜　甫

（712—770）

春夜喜雨

好雨知时节，
当春乃发生。
随风潜入夜，
润物细无声。
野径云俱黑，
江船火独明。
晓看红湿处，
花重锦官城。

A Fine Rain in a Spring Night

A fine rain e'er falls at th' time in craving,
It does timely shower when comes this spring.
Stalking with the breeze into still the night,
It nourished e'erything in a way quiet.
The path in weald is shrouded by clouds dark,
Only the lights from the river boats spark.
I 'hold whither is red and wet at dawn,
Bathed in flowers is Jinguan[①], a grand town.

---

① Jinguan, the ancient name of Chengdu, Sichuan Province.

望 岳

岱宗夫如何？
齐鲁青未了。
造化钟神秀，
阴阳割昏晓。
荡胸生层云，
决眦入归鸟。
会当凌绝顶，
一览众山小。

A View of Mount Tai ①

What Mount Tai in so lofty a hue!
E'en 'yond Qi and Lu ②, you still catch its view.
Wraught by Nature, it is a grandeur wright,
Its front's as if in th' day and rear in th' night.
My heart tides as clouds rise over its crest,
Heave in view birds flying back into th' nest.
When I'll have, one day, ascended its Height,
All hills 'round will look tiny in my sight. ③

---

① **Mountain Tai** a famous mountain located in Shandong Province.

② **Qi and Lu** the two bordering-upon states in the Period of Spring and Autumn, located in nowaday Shandong Province. Mountain Tai straddles the border of Qi and Lu.

③ **When I'll have one day, ascended its Height, All hills' round will look tiny in my sight.** The two lines are a metaphor expression for the poet's lofty aspiration; **its Height**, the crest of Mountain Tai.

夜宴左氏庄

林风纤月落，
衣露净琴张。
暗水流花径，
春星带草堂。
检书烧烛短，
看剑引杯长。
诗罢闻吴咏[①]，
扁舟意不忘。

① 吴咏：指吴歌，这里指古吴国之地的友人之吟唱。

A Night Banquet in Zuo's Abode

Th' crescent's setting into th' woods as blows breeze,
Caught wet are th' livery whose th' lyrist plays.
Th' green water flows by th' path strewn with flowers,
Sparkling over the country cottage are th' spring stars.
I read a book by the aflame candle in shine,
And gaze the sword while drinking sweet wine.
Having heard a crony of Wu① recites a rime,
I 'call a man who fled by a boat in old time②.

---

① **Wu** an ancient state in Spring and Autumn Period, located in nowaday Jiangsu, Anhui an Zhejiang, here referring to this region.

② In the end of Spring and Autumn Period (770-476BC), Fan Li (536 BC-448 BC), the Adviser to Goujian (c. 520-465 BC), the King of Yue State, went away, with unkempt hair, from Goujian by a boat, retreating to live in seclusion after Guojian annihilated Wu State reigned by the King Fuchai (c. 528-473 BC).

龙 门

龙门横野断，
驿树出城来。
气色皇居近，
金银佛寺开。
往还时屡改，
川陆日悠哉！
相阅征途上，
生涯尽几回？

Mount Longmen ①

Split'd by th' River's② Mount Longmen lying across the weald,
Trees grow in rank along th' royal road from th' City③.
The imperial hue pervades over the near field,
The golden Buddhist temples stand in majesty.
Many a year's passed since I paid th' visit latest,
While th' River has been still surging day after day.
Looking forward the life journey of my years rest,
How many visits to Mount Longmen can I pay?

---

① **Mount Longmen** that is, the Dragon Gate Mountain, located in the south of Luoyang City. The mountain was unbroken originally and called Long Mouantain (Dragon Mountain). It was cut by rivermen led by Rongyu, an ancient sovereign,in Xia Dynasty, because flood frequently occurred since the Yihe River in the south of the mountain blocked. After it was broken, the river runs through the cut which looks like a gate, after which Longmen Mountain (Dragon Gate Mountain) was named.

② **The River** referring to the Yihe River.

③ **the City** Luoyang, one of the two capitals of Tang Dynasty.

赠李白

秋来相顾尚飘蓬，
未就丹砂愧葛洪。①
痛饮狂歌空度日，
飞扬跋扈为谁雄。

① 葛洪（283—363），字稚川，自号抱朴子，丹阳郡句容（今江苏句容市）人，东晋道教理论家、著名炼丹家和医药学家。

To Li Bai

Autumn has come but you still rove as thistledown,
Failing in alch'my, you let Ge Hong[①], a sage, down.
Singing and drinking with joy, you beguile 'way your days,
O'erbearing, for whom do you put on such 'rrogant ways?

---

① **Ge Hong** (283-263 AD) , an alchemist and pharmacist in ancient China.

春日忆李白

白也诗无敌，
飘然思不群。
清新庾开府，
俊逸鲍参军。
渭北春天树，
江东日暮云。
何时一樽酒，
重与细论文。

Yearning for Li Bai in a Spring Day

Thou art unmatech'd in poetizing artistry,
Being elegant, thou outshinest thy peers.
As fresh as General Yu's is thy poetry
That's also as refined as Staff Bao's verse.
In th' north of Weishui ①, the spring trees grow fine,
In th' east of th' River ②, clouds float at even.
When will we 'gether drink a cup of wine
To talk about poems and verses again?

---

① **the north of Weihui River** the place where the poet then lived.

② **the east of the (Yangtze) River** the place where Li Bai then wandered.

兵车行

车辚辚，马萧萧，
行人弓箭各在腰。
耶娘妻子走相送，
尘埃不见咸阳桥。
牵衣顿足拦道哭，
哭声直上干云霄。
道旁过者问行人，
行人但云点行频。
或从十五北防河，
便至四十西营田。
去时里正与裹头，
归来头白还戍边。
边庭流血成海水，
武[①]皇开边意未已。
君不闻，
汉家山东二百州，
千村万落生荆杞。

① 武，一作“我”。

A Ballad of Chariots

Many a chariot rattles and countless a steed neighs,
Those who go to the front bring bows on their waists,
Setting off the dusts that engulf the Xianyang Bridgé;
Parents and wives see them off in great worry,
Grasping them by clothes and trying to get in their way,
With loud cries that even be heard by souls in hevean may.
A passenger-by ask one who fares forth: What'shappened?
He answers: "It's too frequent for conscription.
A lad at fifteen is dispatched to guard th' north borderland,
Then at his forty to west to reclaim wasteland.
Th' minor's① head's swathed to sham an adult when he left away,
Aft back, he's again sent to garrison th' bound though hair gray
Become a sea of blood 'cause of war has the border region,
But Emperor Wu② is still high on land expansion.
Haven't you heard:
On th' east of Mount Huashan, in th' two hundred prefectures,
Thousands of villages o'ergrown with brambles and briers.

---

① **minor** juvenile.

② **Emperor Wu** an emperor of Han Dynasty named Liu Che, here is used as a substitution of the emperor of the poet's contemporary.

纵有健妇把锄犁，
禾生陇亩无东西。
况复秦兵耐苦战，
被驱不异犬与鸡。
长者虽有问，
役夫敢申恨？
且如今年冬，
未休关西卒。
县官急索租，
租税从何出？
信知生男恶，
反是生女好。
生女犹得嫁比邻，
生男埋没随百草。
君不见，青海头，
古来白骨无人收。
新鬼烦冤旧鬼哭，
天阴雨湿声啾啾！

E'en if there're stout women farm the field with their sweats,
They crop few because it's infested with too many weeds.
Though these soldiers enlisted from Chin are hard-bearing and tough,
They're still driven away as if chicks and dogs run off.
Your Honor show concern for us with kind inquiry,
But how can I dare repine at th' authority?
For this winter as you just have seen,
In west of th' Pass[①], the conscription's done again!
And also the magistrates urge folks to pay for land renting,
But how can they pay it 'cause of poor cropping?

Who knows it, to have a lad, will bring such an adversity?
Instead, it is luck to have a lass.
A daughter can marry a son of her adjacency.
But a son as if he's engulfed in the grass.
Don't you see
Remained have unburied white bones strewn there and here
Through ages on the Qinghai frontier?
The innocent souls both past and present haunt far and nigh,
And wail aloud, making us heart-bro'en, 'neath the rainy sky!"

---

① **The Pass** referring to Hangu Pass.

前出塞九首（其六）

挽弓当挽强，
用箭当用长。
射人先射马，
擒贼先擒王。
杀人亦有限，
列国自有疆。
苟能制侵陵，
岂在多杀伤。

Song of the West Frontier (Nine Poems, No. VI)

When plying a bow, you'd choose the one strong,
When shooting an arrow, you'd pick the one long.
Shoot his steed first if you aim to th' en'my,
Take th' chief first if you want to his army.
Slaughter should be checked e'en in th' battle line,
The border 'twixt countries is perforce defin'd.
As long as we can resist th' invaders,
Why must we masscre all their soldiers?

前出塞九首(其七)

驱马天雨雪,
军行入高山。
径危抱寒石,
指落层冰间。
已去汉月远,
何时筑城还。
浮云暮南征,
可望不可攀。

Song of the West Frontier (Nine Poems, No. VII)

We ride steeds 'head, braving snow in vastness,
The army marches into mountains lofty.
We ply stones on th' risk trail to make fortress,
Our fingers seem froz'ned off to ice chilly.
The front's away from our hometown far cry,
When will we finish th' forts and go home then?
Clouds over our head towards the south fly,
We crave to ride them 'turn home, but in vain.

城西陂[1]泛舟

青蛾皓齿[2]在楼船，
横笛短箫悲远天。
春风自信牙樯[3]动，
迟日[4]徐看锦缆牵。
鱼吹细浪[5]摇歌扇[6]，
燕蹴[7]飞花落舞筵[8]。
不有小舟能荡桨，
百壶那送酒如泉？

---

① 西陂（bēi）：渼陂，古代湖名，在今陕西户县西。
② 青蛾皓齿：青黛画的眉毛和洁白的牙齿，代指美人。
③ 牙樯：用象牙装饰的帆樯。
④ 迟日：春日，语出《诗经·豳风·七月》："春日迟迟"。
⑤ 鱼吹细浪：细浪好像由鱼儿口中吹出。系夸张手法。
⑥ 歌扇：古代歌舞者手中持的锦扇，一种歌舞道具。
⑦ 蹴：踩，踏。
⑧ 舞筵：跳舞时铺在地上的席子或地毯。筵，竹席。

Boating on Meibei Lake

Alme fairs are singing and dancing on the grand boat,
Gloomy tune of fife and flute into high sky float.
Blown by spring breeze, th' sail on ivory-dight'd mast flies,
The boat adorned with fair riggings slowly plies ①.
Fishes puff out ripples in which mirrored are th' singers' fans,
Swallows flutter petals that fall on th' mat of dance.
How could the nobles enjoy a flood of wines to make merry
On th' grand boat if they were not consigned ② by a wherry?

---

① **ply** sail forward along a certain direction.

② **consign** ship; convey; supply.

后出塞五首（其二）

朝进东门营[①]，
暮上河阳桥[②]。
落日照大旗，
马鸣风萧萧。
平沙列万幕，
部伍[③]各见招。
中天悬明月，
令严夜寂寥。
悲笳[④]数声动，
壮士惨不骄。
借问大将谁？
恐是霍嫖姚[⑤]。

---

① 东门营：军营名，位于洛阳东门，故曰“东门营”。
② 河阳桥：在河南孟津县黄河上的一座浮桥，系晋代杜预所造。
③ 部伍：部队。因为要宿营，所以部队分头集合宿营。
④ 悲笳：低沉严肃的静营之号。
⑤ 嫖姚：同“剽姚”，指西汉大将霍去病。霍去病曾以“嫖姚校尉”一战成名。

Song of the East Frontier[①] (Three Poems, No. II)

Into the East Gate Camp[②] at dawn we enter
And step over Heyang Bridge at vesper.
The setting sun shines over the flags flying,
Steeds neigh aloud up the winds whistling.
Thousands an army tent on the sands anchors,
Each of companies venues its own soldiers.
In th' firmament vast hangs the waxed moon bright,
Under th' strict order th' camp is silent at night,
But we hear th' bugle sound sadly time and again,
The warriors become stern instead of being vain.
I wonder who is the commander of th' army?
A man who's like General Huo[③], it must be.

---

① This poem was written in a tone of a newly enlisted soldier to narrate his adventure of life in barracks.

② **the East Gate Camp** a camp which is located at the East Gate of Luoyang City.

③ **General Huo** Huo Qùbing, a renowned military officer in West Han Dynasty.

月　夜[①]

今夜鄜州[②]月，
闺中只独看。
遥怜小儿女，
未解忆长安。
香雾云鬟湿，
清辉玉臂寒。
何时倚虚幌[③]，
双照[④]泪痕干。

---

① 这是安史之乱期间被囚禁于长安的杜甫写给守在鄜州家中妻子的一首诗。
② 鄜（fū）州：今陕西省富县。当时诗人家属在鄜州的羌村，杜甫被禁于长安。
③ 虚幌：透明的窗帷。幌，帷幔。
④ 双照：与上面的“独看”相呼应，表达对未来团聚的期待。

A Moonlit Night[①]

Tonight over Fuzhou[②] the moon shines bright,
Alone you see Her from th' window of bower,
And yearn for me confined 'n Chang'an[③] all th' night,
Which our children're too young to know better.
Your cloud-like hair is wet by th' balmy dew,
The moon beams make it cold your arms tender.
When will we stand by th' screened window anew
To wipe our tear stains beneath the moon glimmer?

---

① This poem was written to his wife stayed in the home in Fuzhou (Shaanxi Province) by the poet who was confined in Chang'an, the Capital of Tang Dynasty, because of the rebellion launched by An Lushan and Shi Siming.

② **Fuzhou** the place where the poet's family lived at the that moment, while the poet was confined by the rebel troops in Chang'an, the Capital City of Tang Dynasty.

③ **Yearn for me confined 'n Chang'an** see Note ①.

悲陈陶[1]

孟冬[2]十郡[3]良家子，
血作陈陶泽中水。
野旷天清无战声，
四万义军同日死。
群胡[4]归来血洗箭，
仍唱胡歌饮都市。
都人回面向北啼，
日夜更望官军至。

---

① 陈陶：地名，位于长安西北。

② 孟冬：农历十月。

③ 十郡：秦中地区各郡。

④ 群胡：指安史叛军。古代称边塞少数民族为胡人。安禄山是奚族人，史思明是突厥人，部下也多来自北方少数民族部落。

Sorrow for Chentao

In ten prefectures enlist'd are boys of folk fam'lies,
In early winter they shed blood to marsh in th' fray. ①
Battle shouts have faded on the weald 'neath th' clear skies,
Forty thousand warriors died in battle just in a day.
Reek' d with our boys' blood th' arrows of rebel army
Who come to th' City ② to guzzle, singing th' Tartar song.
All folks in Chang'an towards the north aloud cry
For th' royal troops to come soon all night and day long.

---

① **the Fray** referring to Chentao Battle in which the conscripts as the royal troops led by Fang Guan (房琯) , the Prime Minister, of Tang Dynasty, fighting against the rebel troop led by An Shouzhong, but the royal troop were utterly defeated.

② **the City** Chang'an City, the Capital of Tang Dynasty.

对 雪

战哭多新鬼，

愁吟独老翁。

乱云低薄暮，

急雪舞回风。

瓢弃樽无绿[①]，

炉存火似红。

数州消息断，

愁坐正书空[②]。

---

① 绿：酒，以酒的颜色代指酒。

②《世说新语·黜免》："殷中军被废，在信安终日恒书空作字。"

Gazing at Snow

Weeping are th' souls of soldiers newly died,
I, th' aged, 'lone recite rime with sorrow.
Riotous clouds are hanging low at twilight,
The snow flakes are fluttering as winds blow .
Both my gourd and cup are devoid of wine,
Ember in th' burner's still as red as fire.
Receiving no news for which I e'er pine,
I can but "write" characters in the air. ①

---

① **I can but "write" characters in the air** Allusion is adopted from *A New Account of Tales of the World · Dismission*. It expresses the poet's sorrow and despair because of his war-torn country trampled by the rebel troops.

春 望

国破山河在，
城春草木深。
感时花溅泪，
恨别鸟惊心。
烽火连三月，
家书抵万金。
白头搔更短，
浑欲不胜簪。

A View of Spring

Th' state's perished ①, still remain the hills and ri'ers,
In th' spring, grasses in the City ② rankly grow.
Fazed by the hard times, e'en flowers shed tears,
Loath to see folks part their homes ③, birds lost in woe.
Till th' late spring been going on has th' battle bitter ④,
A home letter's worth myriad a piece of gold.
My grey hair's now turned shorter and thinner
That even a hairpin it's unable to hold.

---

① **Th' state's perished** referring the event that Chang'an, the Capital City of Tang Dynasty was captured by the rebel troops headed by An Lushan and Shi Siming, and then the Administration reigned by Emperor Xuanzong (Li Longji) perished in February, 756 AD; the Emperor who was escorted by his kin and kith as well as his confidants fled away.

② **the City** Chang'an, the capital of Tang Dynasty.

③ **folks (to) part their homes** people were coerced to flee from their hometown because of the war waged by the rebel troops.

④ **the battle bitter** the inverted order of "the bitter battle", referring the civil war waged from the winter of 755 AD by the rebels led by An Lushan and Shi Siming.

得舍弟消息二首（其一）

近有平阴[1]信，
遥怜舍弟存。
侧身千里道，
寄食一家村。
烽举新酣战，
啼垂旧血痕。
不知临老日，
招得几人魂。

① 平阴：山东省平阴县。

Receiving a Letter from a Younger Brother

(Two Poems, No. I)

I receive a letter sent from Pingyin lately,
It tells me my brothers ① still 'live, eschewing th' fray ②.
Off being caught, he covers far long a journey
To lodge in a small village thousand miles away.
Bacons rise, going on are the battles bitter,
Everywhere are shedding blood and tears.
I know not how many times I'll see my brother
In th' lease that my life is coming to its late years.

① **one of the poet's brother** referring to Du Ying.

② **eschewing the fray** escaping from the battles (during the civil war waged by the rebel troops led by An Lushan and Shi Siming).

得舍弟[①]消息二首(其二)

汝懦归无计，
吾衰往未期。
浪传乌鹊喜，
深负鹡鸰诗[②]。
生理何颜面，
忧端且岁时。
两京三十口，
虽在命如丝。

① 这里指诗人四个弟弟之一杜观。

② 鹡鸰诗:喻指为兄弟危难而着急。《诗经·小雅·常棣》:“脊令(鹡鸰)在原,兄弟急难。”鹡鸰，一种水鸟。

Receiving a Letter from a Younger Brother①

(Two Poems, No. II)

Neither you will come home 'cause of timidity,
Nor shall I go to see you 'cause of senil'ty.
Though magpies' singing② heard, I'm still in great worry
As what's said in *Wagtail Song* from *Book of Poetry*③.
'Tis so shameful for me to live in such a plight,
I am, all the year, plagued with so great a blight.
Thirty members of our fam'ly in th' two Cities④
Are on th' verge of death 'cause of grave miseries.

---

① **a younger brother** here referring to one of the poet's four brothers, Du Guan.

② **magpie's singing** In Chinese traditional legend, when one hears a magpie sings, he will receive good news or gain fortunes.

③ **As what's said in *Wagtail Song* from *Book of Poetry*** It goes in *Wagtail Song:* A wagtail is out of water, his fellows are much worrier. The poet recited this line as a metaphor for his worry about the fate of his younger brother.

④ **Two Cities** two capital cities, Chang'an and Luoyang in Tang Dynasty.

喜达行在所[①]（其二）

愁思胡笳夕，
凄凉汉苑春。
生还今日事，
间道暂时人。
司隶章初睹，
南阳[②]气已新。
喜心翻倒极，
呜咽泪沾巾

① 行在所：唐肃宗李亨在灵武即位建立的临时朝廷。
② 南阳：这里用东汉光武汉帝刘秀起兵及友莽之地南阳代指李亨的行在所。

Delight for Arriving at the Interim Court

(Two Poems, No. II)

Th' state's perished ①, still remain the hills and ri'ers,
In th' spring grasses in th' City ② rankly grow.
Feazed by th' hard times, even flowers shed tears,
Birds're, when 'hold me part'd my kin, lost in woe.
The new Court in Nanyang assumes a fresh hue,
The doctrine and regime in its rudiment is to brew.
I'm so delight'd that I can't but check my feeling,
Shedding my tears down my face 'cause of joying.

---

① Th' state's perished referring the event that Chang'an, the Capital City of Tang Dynasty was captured by the rebel troops headed by An Lushan and Shi Siming, and then the Administration reigned by Emperor Xuanzong (Li Longji) perished in February, 756 AD. The emperor who, with his kin and kith as well as his confidants, fled away.

② the City, Chang'an, the capital of Tang Dynasty.

月

天上秋期近，
人间月影清。
入河蟾[1]不没，
捣药兔长生。
只益丹心苦，
能添白发明。
干戈知满地，
休照国西营。

① 蟾：蟾蜍，传说中月宫中和玉兔一样的神话动物。常作为月亮的别称。

The Moon

In heaven, the autumn will alight soon,
In th' human world, shining is the clear moon.
The Toad ① sinks not e'en if goes in th' River ②,
Th' Hare ③ ever pounds herbs into elixir.
The bright moon has me fall in misery
And makes my newly grayed hair shiny
The war flames now are rising here and there,
Th' moon! you'd not shine o'er th' west camps of Empire ④

---

① **the Toad** In Chinese myth, it is also a fairy animal that accompanies with the fairy beauty Chang'e in the Moon Palace. Here is a metaphor expression implying that the moon still shining even if mirrored in a river.

② **the River** here referring to the Sky River.

③ **the Hare** In Chinese myth, it is a fairy animal that accompanies with Chang'e who's the fairy beauty in the Moon Palace. He ever pounds herbs into elixir pills which one takes will be immortal.

④ **Th' moon! you'd not shine on west camps of Empire** Otherwise, the soldiers miss their home when seeing the bright moon.

独酌成诗

灯花何太喜，
酒绿正相亲。
醉里从为客，
诗成觉有神。
兵戈犹在眼，
儒术岂谋身。
共被微官缚，
低头愧野人[①]。

① 野人：这里指普通人，特别是没有官位的布衣。

Crooning a Poem While Drinking Alone

What's of delight about the lamp snuff? ①,
I'd rather enjoy the wine in my cup.
I ever drink high wherever I roam,
Aided by Muse ②, I can coin a poem.
Fraught'd with far and nigh are flames of waring,
How can scholarism make one earn a living?
Restrained by the low title of officer,
I feel ashamed to the rank and filer ③.

---

① In Chinese traditional mores, lamp snuff was believed to be a auspicious sign when it appeared. Obviously, the poet did not believe it.

② **Muse** the goddess in charge of poetizing.

③ **the rank and filer** referring to the ordinary folks, especially to those with no title of official position.

羌村三首（其一）

峥嵘赤云西，
日脚下平地。
柴门鸟雀噪，
归客千里至。
妻孥[①]怪[②]我在，
惊定还拭泪。
世乱遭飘荡，
生还偶然遂！
邻人满墙头，
感叹亦歔欷[③]。
夜阑[④]更秉烛，
相对如梦寐。

---

① 妻孥：妻女。
② 怪：惊。
③ 歔（xū）欷（xī）：哽咽、悲泣之声。
④ 夜阑：深夜。更（gèng）：夜深当去睡，今反高烧蜡烛，所以说“更”。这是因为万死一生，久别初逢，过于兴奋，不忍去睡，也不能入睡。

Qiangcun Village (Three Poems, No. I)

The hill-like rosy clouds float 'neath west sky,
The feet of th' sun ① stretch on to the vast plain.
A flock of birds at th' fence gate cry aft cry,
When I come home from far'way land alien.
Startled I'm alive are my children and wife,
Being collected, tears they begin to shed.
I've roved at th' trouble times for half a life,
'Tis by cold luck that I could come back.
Neighbors climb th' walls so that see me they might.
They are greatly pleased and with tears their eyes brim;
The candle shines bright at such the dead of night,
We face to face as if we'd meet in a dream.

---

① **The feet of the sun** a metaphor expression. Like the feet of man, the rays through the clouds cast upon the earth.

曲江二首（一）

一片花飞减却春，
风飘万点正愁人。
且看欲尽花经眼，
莫厌伤多酒入唇。
江上小堂巢翡翠，
苑边高冢卧麒麟。
细推物理须行乐，
何用浮荣绊此身。

The Qujiang River[①] (Two Poems, No. I)

A few of petals fall, taking off th' hue of spring,
A flood of them shed, making me lost in sorrow.
Beholding a host of flowers that are fading,
I'd rather drink still, caring not so great a woe.
Kingfishers nest in th' bower at the ri'er causeway,
Ere grand tomb by Lotus Garden unicorns[②] lie.
Complying with nature, we'd make merry as we may,
Why shall we earn the vainglory that does us tie?

① **the Qujiang River** a artificial river, also called the Qujiang Pool, a resort in Chang'an city.
② **Unicorns** the unicorns that are carved with stone.

曲江二首（其二）

朝回日日典春衣，
每日江头尽醉归。
酒债寻常行处有，
人生七十古来稀。
穿花蛱蝶深深见，
点水蜻蜓款款飞。
传语风光共流转，
暂时相赏莫相违。

The Qujiang River (Two Poems, No. II)

Aft 'turning from levee, I pawn my spring costume
To get wine e'eryday, by ri'er drink high then home.
'Tis no surprise I owe the wineshops here and there,
While for one to live to seventy, through ages 'tis rare.
Amid thick flowers butterflies gaily flutter,
Flying as if dancing, dragonflies flirt with water.
Will you both take a message to spring with which I'll stay?
E'en 'joy it for a while, let it not slip away.

曲江对酒

苑外江头坐不归，
水精宫殿[①]转霏微。
桃花细逐杨花落，
黄鸟时兼白鸟飞。
纵饮久判[②]人共弃，
懒朝真与世相违。
吏情更觉沧洲[③]远，
老大徒伤未拂衣[④]

① 水精宫殿：水晶宫殿，指芙蓉苑中的宫殿。
② 判（pān）：甘愿。
③ 沧州：水畔绿洲，借指归隐之地。
④ 拂衣：拂衣而去，指辞官归隐。《新五代史 · 一行 · 郑遨传》：“见天下已乱，有拂衣远去之意。”

Drinking by the Qujiang① River

Rather than go home, I sit 'lone by the Qujiang Ri'er,
The image of palaces crystal② now looks blear.
Peach flowers are shedding and catkins floating,
Yellow birds with white ones are together flying.
Caring not being loathed, I'm drinking here all the day,
I'm in sloth of levee, which does breach th' routine's way.
Dressing in robe③, I feel 'far fom th' hermitagè,
I will regret when ag'd if not resign early.

---

① **Qujiang River** see the note ① of *The Qujiang River*.

② **The crystal palaces** the grandeur palaces by Qujiang River.

③ **dressing in robe** wearing official uniform, meaning that the poet kept a post in the court.

曲江对雨

城上春云覆苑墙，
江亭晚色静年芳。
林花著雨胭脂湿，
水荇牵风翠带长。
龙武新军深驻辇，
芙蓉别殿谩焚香。
何时诏此金钱会，
暂醉佳人锦瑟旁。

Aft a Rain over Qujiang River

The spring clouds over the Lotus Garden ① hover,
The ri'er tower is bathed in tranquil at vesper.
The flourishing red blooms are all caught wet in rain,
Caressing by wind, water plants make a belt green.
The guards-ward'd carriage now is abandon'd,
Few pilgrims visit th' temples in Lotus Garden.
When will I be 'gain summoned to 'ttain a feast here
To drink till drunk beside the harp of a fair?

---

① **Lotuse Garden** a imperial garden in Tang Dynasty.

遣兴三首（其二）

蓬[①]生非无根，
漂荡随高风。
天寒落万里，
不复归本丛。
客子[②]念故宅，
三年门巷空。
怅望但烽火，
戎车满关东[③]。
生涯能几何，
常在羁旅中。

---

① 蓬：草名，秋枯根拔，风卷而飞，故名飞蓬。常用来比喻游子漂泊不定。
② 客子：客居他乡的人。杜甫自谓。
③ 关东：地名，指函谷关以东地区。

Written on Whim (Two Poems, No. II)

Although floating in the air with wind high,
Thistledown is not as it no root shows.
Falling here and there beneath chilly sky,
It no longer comes back where it grows.
In my roving days, e'er 'bout my hometown I care,
Where my abode remains void for three years.
I look afar with sorrow and beacon fill th' air,
And chariots're bristled with northeast frontiers.
How greatly limited is the lifetime of a man,
But he is often on th' journey in th' land alien.

遣兴三首（其三）

昔在洛阳时，
亲友相追攀。
送客东郊道，
遨游宿南山。
烟尘阻长河，
树羽成皋间。
回首载酒地，
岂无一日还？
丈夫贵壮健，
惨戚非朱颜。

Written on Whim (Two Poems, No. Ⅲ)

When I lived in Luoyang in the past days,
My kin and kith ever made up to me.
I oft saw guests off to th' east suburb ways,
Even with them to South Mountain to sightsee.
The warflames impede th' way of the River, ①
The East Gate's ② fraughted with flags and banners.
Recalling th' haunt where I host'd a dinner,
I wonder if I'll one day return thither.
What's vital for man is healthy body,
He'll lose fair looks if he's lost 'to misery.

---

① the River here referring to the Yangtze River.

② The East Gate the East Gate of Luoyang City.

梦李白二首（其二）

浮云终日行，
游子久不至。
三夜频梦君，
情亲见君意。
告归常局促，
苦道来不易。
江湖多风波，
舟楫恐失坠。
出门搔白首，
若负平生志。
冠盖满京华，
斯人独憔悴。
孰云网恢恢，
将老身反累。
千秋万岁名，
寂寞身后事。

Meeting Li Bai in Dreams (Two Poems, No. II)

As 'drift a cloud is flying all the day,
Thou rare comest back as thou rov'st far way.
But I've dreamt of thee in three a night,
For being eager to meet thee with cordial heart:
Thou art reluctant and restless to go,
" 'Tis hard for me to come," repinest thou.
"Th' river's fraughted with wind and breaker,
My boat may be wrecked in th' journey, I fear."
Going out th' gate, thou scratchest thy gray hair,
As if sighing for not living to thy desire.
Many men in th' Capital are in high place,
While thou hast gained no post with grace.
Who says that grinds slowly the God's mill? ①
But thou art wronged e'en when thou gottest aged still.
Though thou wilt depart from this world 'lonely,
Last fore'er will thy fame sublime and lofty!

---

① The line is a metaphor expression that means everyone will be equally treated under the imperial grace.

秦州[1]杂诗二十首（其七）

莽莽万重山，
孤城山谷间。
无风云出塞，
不夜月临关。
属国[2]归何晚，
楼兰[3]斩未还。
烟尘一怅望，
衰飒正摧颜。

① 秦州：今甘肃天水市。

② 属国：官职名称，亦称典属国，负责处理边疆少数民族部落关系事务等。秦置，西汉沿用，类似于现在的外交部部长。这里代指出使西域的使者。

③ 楼兰：汉时西域国名。汉昭帝时，楼兰与匈奴和好，不亲汉朝。傅介子至楼兰，斩其王首。这里用楼兰代指与唐为敌的吐蕃。

Twenty Poems about Qinzhou① (Twenty Poems, No. VII)

Many a mountain stands monstrous and lofty,
Among the valleys of them seats a lone city.
Clouds fly out of the Pass even no winds blow,
Ere nightfall th' moon shines over the frontier aglow.
Shuguo②, an envoy, who was sent to th' tribe alien
To kill its chief as Fu did in Loulan③, not return'd.
I take a look at th' war flames afar with great woe,
From my face, the desolate autumn takes off hue.

① **Qinzhou** a city in Qinhai Province, located in west frontier, nowday Tianshui City, Qinhai Provine.

② **Shuguo** a title of officer in charge of foreign affairs with the adjacent aliens. He was sent to kill the chief of the recalcitrant alien tribe, learning after Fu Jiezi who was sent to Loulan and beheading its chief and returned during Han Dynasty.

③ **Loulan** a tribe in west border of Han Dynasty, here is a substitution for a alien tibe in Tang Dynasty.

月夜忆舍弟

戍鼓[①]断人行[②]，
边秋[③]一雁声[④]。
露从今夜白[⑤]，
月是故乡明。
有弟皆分散，
无家问死生。
寄书长不达，
况乃未休兵。

① 戍鼓：戍楼上用以报时或告警的鼓声。
② 断人行：指鼓声响起后，便开始宵禁。
③ 边秋：一作“秋边”，秋天边远的地方，此指秦州。
④ 一雁：孤雁。古人以雁行比喻兄弟，一雁，比喻兄弟分散。
⑤ 露从今夜白：指在气节“白露”的一个夜晚。

Yearning for My Brothers in a Moonlit Night

Begins the curfew the drum from th' tower,
A swan's honking over th' autumn frontier.
Dews have become clear white since tonight, ①
The moon over the hometown shines more bright.
My brothers are separated throughout,
Where can I inquire 'to their whereabout? ②
I know nowhere my letters to send,
Much more the war ③ has not come to an end.

---

① **Tonight** the night of White Dew Day which is a solar term occurring in the first ten days of September. The poet wrote this poem at this night.

② Because the poet's house near Luoyang .

③ The civil war was waged by the rebel troops led by An Lushan and Shi Siming.

天末怀李白

凉风起天末[①],
君子意如何?
鸿雁[②]几时到?
江湖[③]秋水多。
文章憎命达,
魑魅喜人过。
应共冤魂语,
投诗赠汨罗。

---

① 天末:天的尽头。秦州地处边塞,犹如在天之尽头。当时李白因永王李璘案被流放夜郎,途中遇赦还至湖南。

② 鸿雁:喻指书信。古代有鸿雁传书的说法。

③ 江湖:喻指充满风波的路途。

Yearning for Li Bai at the World's End

At th'world's end rises the chill wind,
Now what about thy frame of mind?
When comes th' swan who brings thy letter? ①
With autumn floods fraughted is th' river.
Fate hates those who talent'd in writing,
Demons like those who make evildoing.
Thou shouldst with the wronged soul ② confer
By offering a poem 'to th' Miluo River ③.

---

① The poet was eager to hear about Li Bai.

② **The wronged soul** referring to Qu Yuan, a patriot and high-rank official of State of Chu during Waring States Period, who drowned himself because of being framed. Li Bai were enduring the plight Qu Yuan once experienced.

③ **the Miluo River** the river in which Qu Yuan drowned himself.

雨 晴

天际秋云薄，
从西万里风。
今朝好晴景，
久雨不妨农。
塞柳行疏翠，
山梨结小红。
胡笳楼上发，
一雁入高空。

The Clear Sky after a Rain

The autumn thin clouds are floating in th' sky,
The high wind is blown from the west far cry.
After a rain it turns clear this morning,
The excessive rain favors the farming.
The willows on the strands are fresh and green,
Red small fruits borne have the sorbs on mountain.
Blowing are th' bugles from th' city tower,
A wild goose springs into the sky on higher.

山　寺

野寺残僧少，

山园细路[1]高。

麝香眠石竹，

鹦鹉啄金桃[2]。

乱水[3]通人过，

悬崖置屋牢。

上方重阁晚，

百里见秋毫。

---

① 细路：登山的小路。

② 金桃：黄桃。

③ 乱水：山中的泉水、溪水。

A Mountain Temple

A few monks in th' fane on th' mountain,
Toward which a winding trail creeps.
Parrots peck the peaches golden,
In the grove of pinks a musk sleeps.
Passengers wade the streams water,
A steady to'er is built on th' steep
It gets late when I 'scend th' tower,
At th' autumn plume of birds I can peep.

遣 怀

愁眼看霜露，
寒城菊自花。
天风随断柳，
客泪堕清笳。
水净楼阴直，
山昏塞日斜。
夜来归鸟尽，
啼杀后栖鸦。

Drowned in Loneliness

I stare at th' chilly dews with sorrow eye,
The mums come into blooming in th' cold town.
The willow sprays are broken by wind high,
Sounds of the flute make me shed my tears down.
Shade of the to'er's imaged in water clear,
The setting sun falls 'hind th' hazy mountain.
All birds alight on th' woods when night draws near,
Only crows, with 'loud cries, so late return.

初　月[①]

光细弦岂上[②]，
影斜轮未安。
微升古塞外[③]，
已隐暮云端[④]。
河汉不改色，
关山空自寒[⑤]。
庭前有白露，
暗满菊花团。

---

① 初月：这里喻指刚刚即位的肃宗皇帝。

② “月本无光，待日照而光生，半则为弦，全乃成望。”（《左传注》）周王褒诗：“上弦如半璧。”

③ 微升古塞外：喻指肃宗在灵武即位。

④ 已隐暮云端：喻指皇帝身边多佞臣。

⑤ 王褒诗：“关山夜月明。”

The Crescent[1]

Rising in sky, the crescent sheds dim light,
She's not waxed , th' shadows are cast askew.
Beyond the ancient fort[2], she's risen slight,[3]
And hiden amid the clouds in dusk hue.[4]
The Milky Way still keeps gleaming bright,
Barren and cold are th' mountains in frontiers.
In th' front of the yard, heavy dews white
Tide upon a cluster of mum flowers.

---

① **the Crescent** here is a metaphor for Emperor Suzong.

② **beyond ancient fort** here referring to Wuling where Emperor Suzong has just enthroned.

③ **has risen slight** a metaphor for the event that the emperor has just enthroned.

④ **the clouds in dusk hue** a metaphor for the evil courtiers around the emperor.

野　望

清秋望不极，
迢遰[①]起曾阴[②]。
远水兼[③]天净，
孤城隐雾深。
叶稀风更落，
山迥[④]日初沉。
独鹤归何晚，
昏鸦已满林。

① 迢遰（dì）：迢递，遥远貌。
② 曾（céng）阴：重叠的阴云。曾，层。
③ 兼：连着。天净：天空明净。
④ 迥：远。

A View of Weald

I can't see the end of autumn clear sky,
Dark clouds now arise beyond the far cry.
Water at skyline merges with hea'en starry,
Steep'd in heavy brume is a lone city.
Yellow leaves fall as blows the wind chill,
The sun is setting 'hind the far green hill.
Why has the lonely crane returned so later?
Crows have flocked on the woods e'erywhither.

送　远[①]

带甲满天地，
胡为[②]君远行！
亲朋尽一哭，
鞍马去孤城[③]。
草木岁月晚，
关河霜雪清。
别离已昨日，
因见古人情。

---

① 该诗虽题似送他人，实际写诗人自己远行时与亲友别离之情及远行路上的景象——社会战乱，秋景萧瑟、本人孤凄，以及回想与亲友分别时的感伤。

② 胡为：为何。

③ 孤城：这指秦州。

Taking a Long Journey ①

Why would you ② rather leave for faraway?
E'erywhere swarm with th' armoured men.
You'll ride a steed to leave for th' hideaway ③,
Having them sadly weep your kith and kin.
The grass and tree wilt in the late of th' year,
The rivers in th' frontier are clad with frost.
Though I part with my kith and kin yester,
As th' elds did, in mawkishness I am lost.

---

① This poem describes whatever he experienced on his journey.

② The poet used the second person to refer to himself.

③ **Hideaway** a distant small town, here referring to Qinzhou City, nowaday Tianshui City, Gansu Province.

蜀 相

丞相祠堂何处寻？
锦官城外柏森森。
映阶碧草自春色，
隔叶黄鹂空好音。
三顾频烦天下计，
两朝开济老臣心。
出师未捷身先死，
长使英雄泪满襟。

The Premier of Shu Kingdom

Where can we find the Shrine of the Prime Minister?
It lies outside Jin'guan①, 'mid cypresses lusher.
Green grass and steps are bathed in the shine of spring,
The golden orioles amid the leaves aloud sing.
The Lord② once paid him three visits for th' future reigns,
As the premier, he, heart and soul, served two Sovrans.③
He died with regret before conquering the foes,
Which e'er 'rouse them to shed tears the later heroes.

---

① **Jin'guan** namely Jin'guan City, an ancient name of Chengdu City, the Capital of Shu State during the Three Kingdoms Period.

② **the Lord** Liu Bei who later was crown to be the Emperor of Shu Kingdom.

③ **Two Sovrans** the founding Emperor of Shu Kingdom, Liu Bei, and his son, the later Emperor, Liu Shan.

宾　至

幽栖地僻经过少，
老病人扶再拜难。
岂有文章惊海内？
漫劳车马驻江干。
竟日淹留佳客坐，
百年粗粝腐儒餐。
不嫌野外无供给，
乘兴还来看药栏。

Receiving a Guest of Honor

Rarely visit'd, I live alone at such a hideaway,
Wan and aged, visits to my friend I hardly pay.
I have no works that make the world greatly amazed,
To drive to call on me at th' riverside you're fazed[1].
You'd stay at my home a day as the guest of honor,
I've to serve you with spare meals that dines a scholar.
If caring not poor caterin' in such a country,
You'll come again, if you like, to see the peony.

① **fazed** bothered.

狂　夫

万里桥西一草堂，
百花潭水即沧浪。
风含翠篠娟娟净，
雨裛红蕖冉冉香。
厚禄故人书断绝，
恒饥稚子色凄凉。
欲填沟壑唯疏放，
自笑狂夫老更狂。

A Man of Arrogance

By th' west of Wanli Bridge ① stands my humble cottage,
I'd rather take Blooms Stream ② as the Canglang River ③.
A breeze caresses th' tender bamboos with fair foliage,
Shedding balm is many a rain-nurtured lotus flo'er.
I receive no letter from my friends who're at high place,
My children look ashen because suffer being hungry.
Coming to th' end of life, I'll no longer care grace,
And laugh at myself who's more, when aged, of 'rrogancy.

---

① **Wanli Bridge** a bridge situated outside of the south gate of Chengdu during the Period of Three Kingdoms, where Zhuge Liang once saw off Fei Yi as an envoy to Kingdom of Wu.

② **Blooms Stream** also called Blooms Pool, located in the north of the poet's cottage.

③ **the Canglang River** a branch of the Hanjiang River, it was a place where celebrities ever retreated. It becomes a metaphor of secluded place. That the poet took Blooms Stream as the Canglang River means he took it as his hermitage.

江　村

清江一曲抱村流，
长夏江村事事幽。
自去自来梁上燕，
相亲相近水中鸥。
老妻画纸为棋局，
稚子敲针作钓钩。
但有故人供禄米，
微躯此外更何求？

A Riverside Village

A clear river winds around the village,
Our life is bathed in peace in the summer.
Swallows come in and out of my cottage,
Gulls boisterous flirt with the clear water.
On a piece of paper my wife draws a chessboard,
To make a fishhook, pounding a needle is my boy.
As long as ’fforded are meals for my living support,
What anything else do I demand but a health body?

云　山

京洛云山外，

音书静不来。

神交作赋客，

力尽望乡台。

衰疾江边卧，

亲朋日暮回。

白鸥元水宿，

何事有余哀。

The Cloud Mountain

The Cloud Mountain is 'yond Luoyang, the capital ①
From which I've e'er been receiving no news at all.
Even the great poets can't apply themselves to write
Poem but to stare at th' hometown on Belv'dere on Height
Living by th' ri'er, I lies in bed 'cause of ailing ②,
Th' kith and kin who call on me has left at e'ening.
White gulls are resting on water of the river,
Why are they on earth uttering so sad whimper?

---

① **Luoyang** one of the two capitals of Tang Dynasty where the poet's home was located.
② **of ailing** of being ailing.

野　老[1]

野老篱前江岸回，
柴门不正逐江开。
渔人网集澄潭[2]下，
贾客船随返照来。
长路关心悲剑阁[3]，
片云何意傍琴台[4]。
王师未报收东郡，
城阙秋生画角哀。

---

① 野老：杜甫自谓。
② 澄潭：指百花潭。
③ 剑阁：指剑门关，位于今四川省剑阁县境内。
④ 琴台：汉司马相如弹琴的地方，位于成都浣花溪北。

A Countryman ①

I wander ere fence on the bending bank of th' river,
Th' askew wattle gate witnesses the winding flows run.
Fishermen spread their nets into th' Blooms Pool's water,
The merchant ships arrive at th' port when setting is th' sun.
I e'er care where's 'yond Sword Pass ② by th' rebel ta'en,
Why does a cloud float towards the Stage of Lyre ③ ?
Th' east's been not retaken by of th' royal batallion,
The bugle sounds with the sorrow from th' city tower.

---

① **Countryman** here the poet referred to himself.

② **Sword Pass** also called Sword Gate (Jianmen), located in Sichuan Province.

③ **Stage of Lyre** the place where Sima Xiangru played lyre, located in Jiange County, Sichuan Province. This line presents a symbolism for the people in north region flee to the south to avoid the conflict resulted from the rebellion launched by An Lushan and Shi Siming.

南　邻[1]

锦里[2]先生乌角巾，
园收芋栗未全贫。
惯看宾客儿童喜，
得食阶除鸟雀驯。
秋水才深四五尺，
野航[3]恰受两三人。
白沙翠竹江村暮，
相送柴门月色新。

① 南邻：诗人草堂南邻朱山人。
② 锦里：指锦江附近的地方。
③ 野航：小船。

My Southern Neighbor

A neighbor of mine by Jinjiang[①] wears a black towel hat,
Reaping nuts and taro in th' garden, he lives in no penury.
I 'hold his children all the time welcome guests with delight,
Birds peck on the gate steps get along with the family.
The autumn water's just half a dozen feet deep in th' river,
The skiff can take only a couple of us for tripping.
Th' village by white shoal and green bamboos vanished 'to vesper,
We're seen off at the wattle gate beneath the moon in rising.

---

① **Jinjiang** the Jinjiang River.

恨 别

洛城一别四千里，
胡骑[①]长驱五六年。
草木变衰行剑外[②]，
兵戈阻绝老江边。
思家步月清宵立，
忆弟看云白日眠。
闻道河阳近乘胜，
司徒[③]急为破幽燕[④]。

① 胡骑：指安史之乱叛军。
② 剑外：剑阁以南，这里指蜀地。
③ 司徒：指李光弼（708—764），营州柳城（今辽宁省朝阳市）人，契丹族。唐朝中期名将，曾作为检校司徒，率军平叛安史之乱。
④ 幽燕：包括今河北北部、辽宁等地的区域，系当时安禄山发动叛乱之地。

Grief for Separation

I've left from Luoyang City four thousand *li* ① away,
The rebel troops have ta'en it for half dozen a year.
Retreating 'yond Sword Gate when th' flora fade away,
I've to live my late years by th' ri'erside ② 'cause of warfare.
Pining for the hometown, I pace in the moonlit night,
Missing brothers, I mope while gazing at clouds in th' day.
I've heard the foe be ta'en in Heyang by our force might'
Led by Marshal Li ③ to conquer Youyan ④ with no stay.

① **li** a Chinese unit of distance, one li equals half a kilometer.

② **the riverside** here referring to the side of Blooms Stream. Also see the poet's A Reverside Village.

③ **Marshal Li** name Li Guangbi (708-764), who, as the top commander, led the troops to conquer the rebel of An Lushan and Shi Siming.

④ **Youyan** a region covering nowaday the north part of Hebei and the most part of Liaoning, where An Lushan and Shi Siming started the rebellion.

村 夜

萧萧风色暮，
江头人不行。
村舂雨外急，
邻火夜深明。
胡羯[1]何多难，
渔樵寄此生。
中原有兄弟，
万里正含情。

① 胡羯：指安史之乱叛军。

A Village Night

The ceaseless breeze is blowing at vesper,
No souls walk on the road of th' riverside.
Mingled are sounds of rice pounding and shower,
The lights of adjacencies spark in th' night.
Th' rebels bring up'on us so grave an 'ffliction,
Like a fisherman, my future years I've to try.
My brothers're fazed with war in central region,
I miss them all the time though they're far cry.

绝句漫兴九首（其五）

肠断江春欲尽头，
杖藜徐步立芳洲。
颠狂柳絮随风去，
轻薄桃花逐水流。

Nine Quatrains Casually Wrtiten (Nine Poems, No. V)

Standing by th' ri'er in late spring, I lost 'to heart in gloom,
Propping with my stick, I ramble on th' islet in bloom.
The nutsy catkins of willow dance as wind blows,
The frivolous peach petals on th' running stream floats.

客 至

舍南舍北皆春水，
但见群鸥日日来。
花径不曾缘客扫，
蓬门今始为君开。
盘飧市远无兼味，
樽酒家贫只旧醅。
肯与邻翁相对饮，
隔篱呼取尽余杯。

Receiving a Guest

Around my cottage in the spring winds the river,
On which a flock of gulls alight everyday.
I used not to sweep the path strewn with grass lusher,
The wattle gate is opened for greeting you today.
Far from town, I have no cates for you to cater,
In penury, I've to give you the home-brewed wine.
Would you like to drink with my neighbor, an old villager?
I'll call him to come to drink with you if you incline.

春　水

三月桃花浪，
江流复旧痕。
朝来没沙尾，
碧色动柴门。
接缕垂芳饵，
连筒灌小园。
已添无数鸟，
争浴故相喧。

The River in Spring

Peach flowers come into blooming in late spring,
The river tides, rising as high as in the last year.
It overflows the tail of sand shoal in th' morning,
My wattle gate is mirror'd in the water clear.
I link strings to dangle th' bait fragrant for fishing,
Irr'gate th' garden with th' bamboo bails as water fetcher.
From far alien land, alarge flock of birds're here coming,
Fluttering, they seems to vie to bath in th' river.

江　亭

坦腹江亭暖，
长吟野望时。
水流心不竞，
云在意俱迟。
寂寂春将晚，
欣欣物自私。
江东犹苦战，
回首一颦眉。

The Riverside Tower

I lie supine in th' warm ri'erside tower,
Reciting *A View of Weald* at leisure.
Flow runs slow as my heart with nothing to vie,
The clouds float as my mind is in a free fly[①].
The spring is going to quietly fade away,
All creatures increase by their own way.
The waris still raging in the east shore,
I get frown when I'm in recalling the yore.

---

① **fly** flight.

落　日

落日在帘钩，
溪边春事幽。
芳菲缘岸圃，
樵爨倚滩舟。
啅雀争枝坠，
飞虫满院游。
浊醪谁造汝，
一酌散千愁。

The Setting Sun

On th' curtain alighting is the sunbeam,
Tranquil pervades around the spring stream.
The flowers're blooming in th' garden on strands,
I cook with firewood beside my boat on th' sands.
Birds are singing and capering on th' boughs,
The flying insects are swarming in th' yards.
Whoe'er does make thee, the liquor mellow?
One cup of it can drown my great woe.

徐　步

整履步青芜，
荒庭日欲晡。
芹泥随燕觜，
花蕊上蜂须。
把酒从衣湿，
吟诗信杖扶。
敢论才见忌，
实有醉如愚。

Rambling

On the grass growing rank, I ramble slow,
The lower sun shines o'er the yard barren.
With mud in its mouth flying is a swallow,
By 'ttenna, bees flirt with flo'er on th' stamen.
I drink till drunk, e'en making my gown wet,
Propped with my stick cane, a poem I croon.
How dare I say envy can from talent get,
I'm blind drunk as if I were a maron.

水槛遣心二首（其二）

蜀天常夜雨，
江槛已朝晴。
叶润林塘密，
衣干枕席清。
不堪祇老病，
何得尚浮名？
浅把涓涓酒，
深凭送此生。

Meditation upon the Riverside Rail (Two Poem, No. II)

It rains last night as usual 'neath th' Shu ① skies,
This morn th' sun shines over th' river railing.
Still wet are th' sprays of dense woods on th' ri'ersides,
My clothes are dry and th' matress refreshing.
I nearly can't bear th' feazing of disease,
Much less seek for high place and fame I may.
Slow pouring th' wine into my cup at ease,
I'm to live my future life in such a way.

① **Shu** an ancient state, located in southwest region of China, including nowaday Sichuan Province, Chongqing Municipality, and parts of Yunnan, Guizhou, Shaanxi, etc.

晚　晴

村晚惊风度，
庭幽过雨沾。
夕阳薰细草，
江色映疏帘。
书乱谁能帙，
怀干可自添。
时闻有馀论，
未怪老夫潜。

Clear Evening Sky after a Rain

High wind blows the villagè at vesper,
The serene yard's moistened by a shower.
Shining over th' grass is the sunset beam,
The bamboo screen is mirror'd in the stream.
I can myself repour the wine 'to cup
But who can tidy my books in chaos up?
I hear gossips about me now and then,
But no one blames me for my reclusion.

江畔独步寻花七绝句（其三）

江深竹静两三家，
多事红花映白花。
报答春光知有处，
应须美酒送生涯。

Viewing Flowers Alone along the Riverside

(Seven Poems, No. III)

A few cottages seat 'mid lush bamboos by th' river,
The charming flowers red or white are in blooming fine.
I know how to repay the spring-granted sweet hour——
To live my future life by right of drinking sweet wine..

赠花卿

锦城丝管日纷纷，
半入江风半入云。
此曲只应天上有，
人间能得几回闻。

To General Hua

Flutes and strings in Jincheng[①] sound e'ery day 'aloud,
The music is floating into both river breeze and cloud.
Such tune can be only played in heaven fair',
To hear it for human being on th' Earth, 'tis rare.

---

① **Jincheng** an alias of Chengdu City, Sichuan Province.

绝　句

江边踏青罢，
回首见旌旗。
风起春城暮，
高楼鼓角悲。

A Quatrain Aft an Outing in Spring ①

Having been for outing in spring by the river,
I ’hold the flag and banner when turning around.
The wind arise over the spring town at vesper,
The drums and bugles in th’ city to’er sadly sound.

① Entitled by the translator.

悲　秋

凉风动万里，
群盗[①]尚纵横。
家远待书日，
秋来为客情。
愁窥高鸟过，
老逐众人行。
始欲投三峡，
何由见两京。[②]

---

① 群盗：指安史之乱之叛军。
② 诗人此时被滞留在梓州。

Sorrow with Autumn

Blowing for thousand miles is the chilly wind high,
The rebel gangsters ① still run amuck far and nigh.
I crave to receive a letter from th' far'way home,
And much pine for my hometown when the autumn's come.
Gazing with sorrow at birds on high flying away,
Though aged, I, with my fellows, fare for the way.
The Three Gorges I at first intend to gain ②,
How and when can I to the capitals attain? ③

---

① **the rebel gangsters** the rebel troops led by An Lushan and Shi Siming.

② **to gain** to get to.

③ The poet was stayed in Zizhou, Sichuan at this moment, and tried, via Three Gorges, to return his home located in Luoyang and Chang'an, the two capitals of Tang Dynasty.

客　夜

客睡何曾著[①]，
秋天不肯明。
卷帘残月影，
高枕远江声。
计拙无衣食，
途穷仗友生。
老妻书数纸[②]，
应悉未归情。

---

① 著：入睡。
② 老妻书数纸：给妻子写了数封信。

Staying the Nights in Zizhou

In th' alien land, I can't fall into sleep on th' night
That seems too long in autumn to break 'to dawning.
When I roll up the screen, th' setting moon heaves in sight,
Head upon th' pillow, I hear 'far th' river surging.
Poorly managing th' means to afford my daily life,
I have to support th' living by aid of th' bosom friend.
I've sent a couple of letters to my beloved wife,
She would know better why I haven't yet returned.

客　亭

秋窗犹曙色，
落木更天风。
日出寒山外，
江流宿雾[1]中。
圣朝无弃物，
老病已成翁。
多少残生事，
飘零任转蓬。

---

① 宿雾：晨雾。

Staying in a Bower

The dawn of an autumn day breaks into th' window,
The trees are shedding their leaves as the winds blow.
The sun rises beyond th' distant mountains chiller,
Amid the mist of early morning surges th' ri'er.
Our court never ditch anyone to serve the Sovran, ①
Merely I've become one of wan and old men.
I've many things to do in th' rest years of my life,
But I've to, as the thistledown, drift to survive.

① Of course, this is an ironical expression.

闻官军收河南河北

剑外忽传收蓟北，
初闻涕泪满衣裳。
却看妻子愁何在，
漫卷诗书喜欲狂。
白首放歌须纵酒，
青春作伴好还乡。
即从巴峡穿巫峡，
便下襄阳向洛阳。

Aft Hearing the News of Recapturing Henan and Hebei

'Yond Sword Gate[①] the news retaking the north of Ji[②] fly,
When heard, with tears down my face I can't but cry,
The sorrow looks of my wife and children soon fades,
I'm exhalted as packing th' books up with casual ways.
Though aged with hair gray, I sing while drinking wine,
With my fam'ly, I'll return home in th' spring days fine.
We'll sail through from Three Gorges along the River,
And th' journey from Xiangyang to Luoyang we'll cover.

---

① **beyond Sword Gate** referring to Sichuan where the poet then lived.

② **the north region of Ji** covering the northern part of Hebei, the whole Liaoning, etc, which was the base of the rebel troops led by An Lushan and Shi Siming. Ji is nowday Beijing.

巴 山[①]

巴山遇中使[②]，
云自陕城[③]来。
盗贼[④]还奔突，
乘舆[⑤]恐未回。
天寒邵伯树[⑥]，
地阔望仙台[⑦]。
狼狈风尘里，
群臣安在哉。

---

① 巴山：当时的阆州，位于今四川省东北部，是唐朝设置的行政区。阆居巴子之国，故曰巴山。

② 中使：宫中派出的使者；多指宦官。《后汉书·宦者传·张让》："凡诏所征求，皆令西园驺密约敕，号曰'中使'。"

③ 陕城：古地名，位于今河南省三门峡市。

④ 盗贼：代指叛军。

⑤ 舆：车。这里指龙辇。

⑥ 邵伯树：《史记·燕召公世家》："召公之治西方，甚得兆民和。召公巡行乡邑，有棠树，决狱政事其下，自侯伯至庶人各得其所，无失职者。召公卒，而民人思召公之政，怀棠树不敢伐，歌咏之，作《甘棠》之诗。"棠树："今之棠梨树也。"（张守节正义），后因此称棠梨树为"邵伯树"。邵伯：周召公奭，因封地在召，故称召公或召伯，又作邵公、邵伯。

⑦ 望仙台：望仙台是唐大明宫内道教建筑。据文献记载，唐武宗痴迷道教神仙之术，于会昌年间修筑。

Bashan Mountain

I met a royal envoy in th' Bashan Region ①,
He said he came hither from Shaancheng City ②
Where still overrun the gangsters of rebellion,
Returned maybe not has th' imperial carriagè ③.
The Tree of Shaobo ④ still stands in th' cold weather,
The Stage for Watching Fairy erects in th' field wide.
Like frightening rats, the courtiers soon scamper,
Wherever those who are pillars ⑤ of the court hide?

---

① **Bashan Region** the Prefecture of Langzhou in Tang Dynasty, located the north part of Sichuang Province.

② **Shaancheng** the name of an ancient town, which was the center of Shaanshou, located in the nowaday Sanmenxia City, Henan Province.

③ The emperor fled out of the capital because of the attack by the rebel troops.

④ **Tree of Shaobo** a kind of cherry-apple tree in Shaanzhou, later it was called Tree of Shaobo in memory of Shaobo (Master Zhao) for his virtue and merit.

⑤ **Pillars** a metaphor for the courtiers who were rendered as the backbones of the country.

岁　暮

岁暮远为客，
边隅还用兵。
烟尘犯雪岭，
鼓角动江城。
天地日流血，
朝廷谁请缨。
济时敢爱死，
寂寞壮心惊。

The End of the Year

I still rove in the alien land at th' end of th' year,
The battle's still going on in the faraway frontier.
The enemy troops of Tartar invade Snow Peak,
The sounds of drums and bugles make Jiangcheng ① shake.
Bloods are shedding day and night 'neath th' air gloomy,
Who'll ask for an Order to combat with en'my?
How can I fear death to put the turmoil into peace
Though in lonely hide'way, tides in my heart ne'er cease?

① **Jiangcheng** here referring to Zizhou where the poet then stayed.

暮　寒

雾隐平郊树，
风含广岸波。
沉沉春色静，
惨惨暮寒多。
戍鼓犹长击，
林莺遂不歌。
忽思高宴会，
朱袖拂云和。

A Chilly Evening

The trees on the weald hide in mist,
Off the shore the winds raise breaker.
Dreariness makes the spring whist,
Dourness get it more cold at vesper.
Th' war drums beat again and again,
Orioles fall silent 'cause of fright.
A feast once held I recalled amain,
Fair hands playing strings imaged in sight.

渡　江

春江不可渡，
二月已风涛。
舟楫欹斜疾，
鱼龙偃卧高。
渚花兼素锦，
汀草乱青袍。
戏问垂纶客，
悠悠见汝曹。

Crossing the River

The spring river now can't be crossed over,
In the midspring winds raise many a breaker.
Boats are sailing on th' ri'er in a swift way,
Fishes jump up as high as the causeway.
Like white silk are the blooms upon the shoal,
Seem the black robe ① does the grass on the shore.
I ask th' fisherman in a joking manner,
Why are you so carefree and leisure?

---

① **black robe** the livery of the lower-rank officials in Tang Dynasty.

登 楼

花近高楼伤客心，
万方多难此登临。
锦江春色来天地，
玉垒浮云变古今。
北极朝廷终不改，
西山寇盗莫相侵。
可怜后主还祠庙，
日暮聊为梁甫吟。

Ascending a Tower

Seeing flowers near the tower, I lost in bro'en heart, ①
I 'scend'd it just at th' time when the country at stake.
The spring hues over Jinjiang ② on the earth alight,
Th' world ever changes as th' clouds float over Mount Jade,
Like Polaris, our court's e'er-lasting and divine,
How dare you Tatar rebels invade our land, 'tis in vain!
Even the Late Emperor Liu ③ had his shrine!
I 'cite *Song of Liangfu* ④ to drown my woe at even.

---

① Why did the the poet lost in broken heart? Because his country sufferred a turmoil raised by the rebellion.

② **Jinjiang** a river located near the Humble Cottage of the poet in Chengdu, Sichuan Province.

③ **the Late Emperor Liu** i.e. Liu Shan, the son and the successor of Liu Bei, the founding emperor of Shu Kingdom during the period of Three Kingdoms. He was believed as an imbecile emperor in Chinese history.

④ ***Song of Liangfu*** a kind of *Yuefu* Poem in ancient China, here the poet used it as a substitution for the present poem of his own.

归 雁

东来万里客[①]，
乱[②]定几年[③]归？
肠断江城[④]雁，
高高向北飞。

① 万里客：作者自谓。
② 乱：指安史之乱。
③ 几年：几时，何时。
④ 江城：这里指梓州。

The Returning Swan

How many years th' state will be put into order
So that return hometown in east far① can a rover②?
A swan③ in Jiangcheng, who's lost into broken heart,
Can at ease return northwards afar in high flight.

---

① The poet's hometown seated Luoyang, in the east to Chengdu.

② **a rover** that which the poet referred to himself.

③ **a swan** here is a metaphor for the poet himself.

绝句二首（其一）

迟日[1]江山丽，
春风花草香。
泥融飞燕子，
沙暖睡鸳鸯。

① 迟日：春日。

Two Quatrains (No. I)
——A Spring View ①

The rill and hill are dressed in beauty in spring,
Caressed by mild breeze, flowers shed fragrance.
Swallows fly with mud in their beaks for nesting
Mandarin ducks are sleeping on the warm sands.

① The subtitle is attached by the translator.

绝句二首（其二）

江碧鸟逾白，
山青花欲燃。
今春看又过，
何日是归年。

Two Quatrains (No. II)
——The Meditation in Spring ①

Gulls in white plume fly over the green river,
On th' hill, blooming is the flame-like flower.
The spring of this year will fade' way anon,
Whene'er can I return to my hometown?

① The subtitle is attached by the translator.

绝句六首（其二）

藹藹花蕊乱，
飞飞蜂蝶多。
幽栖身懒动，
客至欲如何。

Six Quatrains (No. II)
——Being in Sloth [1]

Coming 'to blooming is many a flo'er,
Around which butterflies and bees flutter.
Being in sloth, I'd rather at ease stay home,
What can I do if a guest doses come?

① The subtitle is attached by the translator.

绝句四首（其三）

两个黄鹂鸣翠柳，
一行白鹭上青天。
窗含西岭千秋雪，
门泊东吴万里船。

Four Quatrains (No. III)
——The Early Spring ①

In green willows two orioles cheerfully singing,
A rank of egrets fly toward the vast blue sky.
West Ridge ② snow framed in the window as a painting,
A host of boats from far th' east moor at th' gate nearby.

① The subtitle is attached by the translator.

② **West Ridge** a sow mountain, located in Dayi County, Sichuan Province.

春 远

肃肃花絮晚，
菲菲红素轻。
日长惟鸟雀，
春远独柴荆。
数有关中乱，
何曾剑外清。
故乡归不得，
地入亚夫营。

The Fading Spring

Willows are spitting catkins white 'to skies,
Peaches shedding red petals upon ground.
A flock of birds on the day heave in eyes,
In late spring the wattle gate stands 'round.
Frequent invade Guanzhong ① the foes alien,
When they are driven 'way from'yond th' Sword Gate?
I can't 'turn to my hometown in Central Plain, ②
Instead, 'to Yafu Camp ③ I have to retreat.

---

① **Guanzhong** the Central Shaanxi Plain.

② The poet could not return hometown because the warfare forfended his way to his homeland.

③ **Yafu Camp** Zhou Yafu Camp, located in the south of Diandchi Lake.

旅夜书怀

细草微风岸，
危樯独夜舟。
星垂平野阔，
月涌大江流。
名岂文章著，
官应老病休。
飘飘何所似，
天地一沙鸥。

Meditation at Night during a Tour

Breeze caresses the grass on th' shore in green,
My boat's alone moored by riverside at night.
Stars cast their beams over so vast a plain,
Reflect'd in the surging River is the moon bright.
How can one by his works achieve his honor?
When wan and aged, an officer should retire.
For a whole life I've drift'd as a rover
As if a gull flies in the boundless air.

长江二首（其二）

浩浩终不息，
乃知东极[①]临。
众流归海意，
万国奉君心。
色借潇湘阔，
声驱滟滪[②]深。
未辞添雾雨，
接上遇衣襟。

① 东极：东海。
② 滟滪：滟滪堆（大石块堆）。

The Yangtze River (Two Poems, No. II)

Thou surgest and billow'st night and day,
Towards the East Sea runest forever
To which all a river goes its way
As e'eryone submits himself to th' emperor.
Copied from thine is Xiaoxiang's grand scenery, ①
Thy loud sound can drive boulders away.
The rain and mist wet my livery,
Which I do not care, be that as it may.

---

① **Xiaoxiang** here referring to Xiangjiang River.

武侯庙

遗庙丹青落，
空山草木长。
犹闻辞后主，
不复卧南阳。

The Temple of Marquis of Prowess[①]

The paint of the Marquis Temple erodes and peels,
The grass and tree grow rank on the deserted hills.
Echo still his 'dieus to th' Sovran[②] ere a compaign[③],
He'll ne'er return to Nanyang, his hometown, again.

---

① **Marquis of Prowess** Zhuge Liang, the premier of Shu State during Three Kingdoms Period. He was conferred a posthumous title of Marquis of Prowes after he sacrified on the battleground.

② **The Sovran** here referring to the young Emperor, Liu Shan, son of Liu Bei, the founding Emperor of Shu State.

③ **Compaign** wage a war on Wei Kingdom was ready to be waged by Zhuge Liang.

八阵图

功盖三分国，
名成八阵图。
江流石不转，
遗恨失吞吴。

The Eight Battling Array [1]

Widely renowned for the Eight Battle Array,
In Three Kingdoms he made the peerless feast.
The river e'er surges but th' stones [2] still firm stay,
He regret'd for th' war 'nnexing Wu of East [3].

---

① **The Eight Battling Array** an embattling strategical arrangement invented by Zhuge Liang, the Prime Minister of Shu Kingdom during the period of Three Kingdoms.

② **Stones** substitution for the Eight Battle Array due to which is built with stones.

③ **the war annexing Wu of East** a war waged by Liu Bei, the founding Emperor of Shu Kingdom during the Period of Three Kingdoms to try annex Wu Kingdom. Zhuge Liang made affort in persuading the emperor to give up such a campaign but in vain.

江　上

江上日多雨，
萧萧荆楚秋。
高风下木叶，
永夜揽貂裘。
勋业频看镜，
行藏独倚楼。
时危思报主，
衰谢不能休。

Over the River

Over the river, it's raining ceaseless,
Jingchu ① autumn is lost in loneliness.
As high winds blow, the leaves fall on ground,
I e'er hold the wardrobe all night around. ②
With no feat, I look 'to mirror in ail, ③
What I can do is just to lean on the rail. ④
Craving to, in th' hard time, repay th' Sovran,
I can't give up though I'm feable and wan.

---

① **Jingchu** the region of ancient Chu State.

② Though the poet craves to serve the Sovran, he is not summoned by the court. "He hold the warrobe all the night" is just a metaphor for showing his eager desire to serve the court.

③ Having no feat worrying about his career, the poet looks into mirror because of his eagerness to make achievements.

④ Not summoned by the court, he is unoccupied with a desire to serve the court, so just lean on the rail to look forward to be summomed.

月　圆

孤月当楼满，
寒江动夜扉。
委波金不定，
照席绮逾依。
未缺空山静，
高悬列宿稀。
故园松桂发，
万里共清辉。

The Waxed Moon

Over th' mansion， th' wax moon lonely shines bright,
The chilly river reflects th' door at night
'Neath th' golden beams flashing on th' rippling water,
Which makes the matress seem much more tender.
'Tis silent in the mountain 'neath th' full moon bright,
And th' sparse stars on high are shedding dim light.
Cassia and pine in hometown sheds fragrance,
I'll share the bright moon with fam'ly in distance.

宿江边阁

暝色延山径，
高斋次水门。
薄云岩际宿，
孤月浪中翻。
鹳鹤追飞静，
豺狼得食喧。
不眠忧战伐，
无力正乾坤。

Stay for a Night in a Riverside Cabinet①

Dusk creeps along the path of hill high,
Beside the Gate② th' Cabinet stands nearby.
The thin clouds are staying in the Gorge③,
The lonely moon is flashing in the surge.
Cranes begin to rest aft chase each other,
Getting prey, wolves uproar and clamour.
Sleepless, about th' warfare I so worry,
But unable to set it 'to peace our country.

---

① **The riverside cabinet** named West Cabinet which lies in the riverside near Kuimen Gate, a natural scenery of Qutang Gorge, one of the Three Gorges in the upper reach of Yangtze River.

② **The Gate** referring to the entrance pass ——Qutang Pass of Three Gorges. It is also known as the Gate of Kui.

③ **The Gorge** here referring to Qutang Gorge.

吹　笛

吹笛秋山风月清，
谁家巧作断肠声。
风飘律吕相和切，
月傍关山几处明。
胡骑中宵堪北走，
武陵一曲想南征。
故园杨柳今摇落，
何得愁中却尽生。

Fluting

Flute sounds o'er hill, with autumn breeze 'neath th' bright moon,
By whom coined is th' music that makes me heart-bro'en?
The touching tune is, with the fresh wind, flying,
Over mountain in frontier th' moon is shining.
Moved once by such a tuneTartar retreat'd north[①],
Song of Wuling was once play'd in fighting south[②].
In Duling Graveyard[③], shedding leaves are willows,
How can I spend my late years with great sorrows?

---

① **Moved once by such a tuneTartar retreat'd north** Liu Yueshi, also called Liu Kun, a famous army leader of Jin Dynasty, who once besieged by Tartar troops and made them withdraw by blowing flute tune because of which was so touching that Tartar men were moved to retreat to north.

② ***Song of Wuling* was once played in fighting south** Ma Yuan, a famous general in the beginning of East Han Dynasty, who composed and blew a tune of Deep *Wuling Stream* when fighting south. *Song of Wuling* also called *Wuling Stream Deep*.

③ **Duling Graveyard** the tomb of Liu Xun in Chang'an,, an emperor of Han Dynasty, here also a substitution for poet's hometown.

秋风二首（其二）

秋风淅淅吹我衣，
东流之外西日微。
天清小城捣练急，
石古细路行人稀。
不知明月为谁好？
早晚孤帆他夜归。
会将白发倚庭树，
故园池台今是非。

The Autumn Wind (Two Poems, No. II)

The autumn wind blows my clothes with whistling,
Afar from th' ri'er, heaves in sight th' sun in setting.
Beating clothes sound o'er the town 'neath sky fair,
On th' stone-paved path, few pedestrians wander.
I know not whom is favor'd by th' moon bright,
Sailing all th' day, my boat'll reach home at night.
Being aged, to lean on a yard tree I'm eager
But fallen 'to ruins might have th' pool and bower.

秋兴八首（其六）

瞿塘峡[①]口曲江[②]头，
万里风烟[③]接素秋。
花萼[④]夹城[⑤]通御气，
芙蓉小苑[⑥]入边愁。
珠帘绣柱[⑦]围黄鹄[⑧]，
锦缆牙樯[⑨]起白鸥。
回首可怜歌舞地[⑩]，
秦中[⑪]自古帝王州。

---

① 瞿塘峡：三峡之一，在夔州东。
② 曲江：水名，在长安之南。
③ 万里风烟：指夔州与长安相隔万里之遥，战火蔓延各地。
④ 花萼：花萼相辉楼，在长安南内兴庆宫西南隅。
⑤ 夹城：据《长安志》记载，唐玄宗为了潜行曲江，于开元二十年（公元732），从大明宫依城修筑复道，经通化门，达南内兴庆宫，直至曲江芙蓉园。通御气：此复道因系方便天子游赏而修，故曰“通御气”。
⑥ 芙蓉小苑：芙蓉园，也称南苑，在曲江西南。
⑦ 珠帘绣柱：形容曲江行宫别院的楼亭建筑极其富丽华美。
⑧ 黄鹄：天鹅。
⑨ 锦缆牙樯：指曲江中装饰华美的游船。
⑩ 歌舞地：指曲江池苑。此句是说昔日繁华的歌舞之地曲江，如今屡遭兵灾，荒凉寂寞。这借指长安。
⑪ 秦中：指长安。

Meditation in Autumn (Eight Poems, No. VI)

From mouth of Qutang Gorge to head of Qujiang River,
A myriad miles of war smoke with autumn hue spreads o'er.
Th' royal rill runs from Calyx To'er [①] to Lotus Garden [②],
To which the sad news comes from th' frontier now and then.
Swans romp in the lake around which stand pavilions fair,
The ornate boats spring a flock of gulls to fly 'to air.
What's pity for th' deserted haunt once fraughted with balls,
As th' hub of Chin [③], it's e'er many empire's Capitals.

---

① **Calyx To'er** a tower situated in an imperial palace in the south of Chang'an City in Tang Dynasty.

② **Lotus Garden** an imperial garden in Tang Dynasty.

③ **The hub of Chin** here referring to Chang'an which was established as the capitals of many dynasties in China.

咏怀古迹五首（其三）

群山万壑赴荆门，
生长明妃尚有村。
一去紫台连朔漠，
独留青冢向黄昏。
画图省识春风面，
环佩空归夜月魂。
千载琵琶作胡语，
分明怨恨曲中论。

Ode to the Ancestral (Five Poems, No. III)

Crossing thousand a hill and vale, I reach Jingmen Gate,
Thither th'village where born was Princess Ming① still stands.
She 'parted th' Palace and trecked in Nafud desolate,
Beneath the setting sun, her lone tomb now lies in vast sands.
How could a portrait tell her fair looks like th' shine of spring?
In th' night her soul haunts backèd beneath the moon brighter.
Th' pipa tune she once played has been for ages resouding,
It tell us what bitterness and hate she'd to suffer.

---

① **Princess Minig** the would-be concumbine of Emperor Yuan of Han Dynasty but she had not become the real concumbine of the emperor because she was not portraited as her real beauty since she did not bribe the painter, Mao Yanshou. Afterwards, she was allowed to marry to the chief of Xiongnu Tribe in the north frontier. Therefore, she trecked in Nafud.

咏怀古迹五首（其四）

蜀主[①]窥吴幸三峡，
崩年亦在永安宫[②]。
翠华想像空山里，
玉殿虚无野寺中。
古庙杉松巢水鹤，
岁时伏腊[③]走村翁。
武侯祠堂[④]常邻近，
一体君臣祭祀同。

---

① 蜀主：刘备，三国时期蜀国皇帝。

② 永安宫：蜀汉昭烈皇帝刘备托孤的故址，位于今重庆市奉节县。章武二年（222），刘备率四万大军东下，为关羽报仇，遭东吴大将陆逊火攻连营退守鱼复，改县名永安，营亦名永安宫。

③ 伏腊：伏天腊月，指每逢节气村民皆前往祭祀。

④ 武侯祠堂：蜀国丞相诸葛亮祠。

Ode to the Ancestral (Five Poems, No. IV)

Lord of Shu ① waged a war on Wu ② in Three Gorges,
Defeated, in the Yong'an Palace ③ he passed away.
That flags're flyin' in th' mountains now just in vision emerges,
The Palace's lost amidst the temples deserted in the day.
Water cranes nearby nidify on th' old fir and pine,
Villagers go to worship the Sages ④ when comes a fete.
Temple of Zhuge ⑤ is adjacent to his Lord's shrine,
They both enjoy th' sacrifice offered by folks at this date.

---

① **Shu** a kingdom, which is located in southwest region of China, including nowaday Sichuan Province, Chongqing Municipality, and parts of Yunnan, Guizhou, Shaanxi, etc., founded by Liu Bei during Three Kingdoms Period.

② **Wu** a kingdom, which is located in southeast region of China, including nowaday Zhejiang, Fujian, Guangdong, Jiangxi, Hainan, and Shanghai, and parts of Jiangsu, Hunan, and Hubei, founded by Sun Quan during Three Kingdoms Period.

③ **Yong'an Palace** the headquarter of campus on which Liu Bei garrisoned his troops when he waged the war on Wu Kingdom. It is located in the present Fengjie County, Chongqing Municipality.

④ **Sages** referring to the Emperor Liu Bei and his Prime Minister Zhuge Liang.

⑤ **Zhuge**, i.e. Zhuge Liang, the Prime Minister of Shu Kingdom.

阁　夜

岁暮阴阳催短景，
天涯霜雪霁寒宵。
五更鼓角声悲壮，
三峡星河影动摇。
野哭千家闻战伐，
夷歌数处起渔樵。
卧龙跃马终黄土，
人事音书漫寂寥。

Staying a Night in the West Tower

The sun and moon make th' day shorter at th' end of year,
The night becomes colder aft snow at the world's corner.
Drum and bugle sound solemn and stirring at dawn blear,
Stars o'er Three Gorges cast images that flash in th' River[①].
Wails' cause of war sound from all households over th' weald vast,
O'erwhelmed near are th' songs of alien-tribe fishers 'nd woodsmen.
E'en Zhuge[②] and Gongsun[③], two heroes, have turned to dust,
What does it matter I get no letter and live 'lone?

---

① **the River** here referring to the Yangtze River.

② **Zhuge** i.e., Zhuge Liang, the Prime Minister of Shu Kingdom.

③ **Gongsun** i.e. Gongsun Shu,a warlord chief occupied Shu during the beginning of the East Han Dynasty. He was crowned himself as White Emperor.

暮　春

卧病拥塞在峡中，
潇湘洞庭虚映空。
楚天不断四时雨，
巫峡常吹千里风。
沙上草阁柳新暗，
城边野池莲欲红。
暮春鸳鹭立洲渚，
挟子翻飞还一丛。

The Late Spring

I have to stay in Wuxia Gorge 'cause of ill,
Be just images Xiaoxiang and Dongting will. ①
Rains shower ceaseless beneath the Chu sky,
In Wuxia Gorge frequent rise the winds high.
On th' shoal, lush is th' willow by West Tower,
Lotus in th' pond 'by th' town is to flower.
Mandarin ducks and heron ②, either standing
On th' bar or flyin' with their birdlings, in late spring.

---

① **Xiaoxiang and Dongting** Xiangjiang River and Dongting Lake, located in Hunan Province, where the poet would leave for but was delayed because of ill. So they both become images for the poet.

② **Mandarin ducks and heron** both are the migrant birds which northwards fly. In contrast, the poet also wanted to be bound for north, returning his hometown but in vain.

月三首（其一）

断续巫山雨，
天河此夜新。
若无青嶂月，
愁杀白头人。
魍魉移深树，
虾蟆动半轮。
故园当北斗，
直指照西秦。

The Moon (Three Poems, No. I)

Th' rain falls on and off in Wushan Mountain,
But much clear is the Milky Way tonight.
Had not th' moon hung over the hills green,
I'd have lost in broken heart 'cause of plight.
Hide in the woods the demon and monster,
Toad ① wanders around in th' crescent glowing.
I take Chang'an ② as the Big Dipper,
Over the West Chin, the moon is shining.

---

① In Chinese myth, toad is lives in the Moon Palace with Chang'e, a fairy beauty.

② **Chang'an** the capital of Tang Dynasty,where the poet's abode was located.

夜 雨

小雨夜复密，
回风吹早秋。
野凉侵闭户，
江满带维舟。
通籍恨多病，
为郎忝薄游。
天寒出巫峡，
醉别仲宣楼[①]。

① 仲宣楼：为纪念东汉末年诗人王粲在襄阳作《登楼赋》而建，位于襄阳城东南角城墙之上。因王粲字仲宣，故名。

A Night Rain

It is drizzling ceaseless in the dead night,
In the early autumn, winds keep blowing.
Chill penetrates the houses closèd tight,
Th' river tides stay my boat to start sailing.
I'm 'shamed for not serving th' Court right away
Though 'ppointed 'cause of illness and wander.
When it chills, sail 'way from Wuxia ① I may,
I'll then drunkenly 'part from Zhongxuan To'er ②.

---

① **Wuxia** Wuxia Gorge, one of Three Gorges.

② **Zhongxuan Tower** a tower in Xiangyang City. It was built in memory of *Rhapsody on Asceding Tower* which was written by Wang Zhongxuan i.e., Wang Can,(177-217 AD), a famous literateur and officer in the end of East Han Dynasty, in Xiangyan City.

复愁十二首（其十）

江上亦秋色，
火云终不移。
巫山犹锦树，
南国且黄鹂。

Greater Sorrow (Twelve Poems, No. X)

Fair is autumn scene o'er th' river,

The rosy clouds in th' sky still linger.

On Wushan Hill woods're lush growing,

In th' southland orioles're 'loud singing.

晓　望

白帝更声尽，
阳台曙色分。
高峰寒上日，
叠岭宿霾云。
地坼江帆隐，
天清木叶闻。
荆扉对麋鹿，
应共尔为群。

A View of Dawn

Th' drum of th' dawn has ceased in Badi City,
O'er Mount Yangtai ① in sight is th'dawning pale.
Th' sun rises above mountain height chilly,
The haze clouds linger in the vale and dale.
All sails are out of sight in th' grand fissure ②,
I hear the leaves are rustling 'neath sky clear.
I'd be with my kith and kin together,
But live in a humble yard with David's deer.

---

① **Mount Yangtai** also called Mount Wangwu, situated in Jiyuan City, Henan Province and Jincheng City, Shanxi Province.

② **Grand fissure** a metaphor expression for the Yangtze River.

登　高

风急天高猿啸哀，
渚清沙白鸟飞回。
无边落木萧萧下，
不尽长江滚滚来。
万里悲秋常作客，
百年多病独登台。
艰难苦恨繁霜鬓，
潦倒新停浊酒杯。

Ascending the Height

The apes cry up th' high wind beneath th' vast sky,
O'er clear river and white shoal the birds hover high.
Th' autumn woods in vastness shed leaves aft leaves,
The endless Great Ri'er surges waves aft waves.
I e'er rove far from home in th' gloomy autumn chill,
Though wan and aged, I 'lone ascend th' Stage still.
Th' hardship and suffering make my hair white,
I've to give up wine 'cause of being in plight.

冬　至

年年至日长为客，
忽忽穷愁泥杀人。
江上形容吾独老，
天边风俗自相亲。
杖藜雪后临丹壑，
鸣玉朝来散紫宸。
心折此时无一寸，
路迷何处见三秦。

Winter Solstice Day

I ever wander on Winter Solstice Day year aft year,
Never do I get rid of poverty and great sorrows.
Sailing on river, an aged feature only I bear,
Accustom'd to their rite, I get 'long with th' native fellows.
Propped with my stick, I stand by the ditchside after snow,
As if I hear th' tinkling of jade pendants aft levee's o'er.
At such a moment, I lost into th' broken heart with woe,
At sea, when I'll return to serve the court, I wonder.

白帝楼

漠漠虚无里，
连连睥睨侵。
楼光去日远，
峡影入江深。
腊破思端绮，
春归待一金。
去年梅柳意，
还欲搅边心。

The Tower of Baidi City

Beneath the endless and blear sky,
The parapet wall erects extreme high.
Th' setting sun beams are mirror'd on th' tower
Whose shadow's bathed in the deep river.
The silk livery's craved at th' year's end,
Worthy to be a gold is th' spring's advent.
Even the last year wintersweet and willow
Still make me drowned in nostalgia and sorrow.

江边星月二首（其一）

骤雨清秋夜，
金波耿玉绳。
天河元自白，
江浦向来澄。
映物连珠断，
缘空一镜升。
馀光隐更漏[①]，
况乃露华凝。

① 更漏：这里是借代用法，借指黑夜。

Looking at the Moon and Stars by the Riverside

(Two Poem, No. I)

Aft heavy a rain, comes a fresh autumn night,
The golden beam of th' moon vies with the stars'.
The Milky Way all 'long gives off starlight,
The Ri'er ① is all the way clear like a glass,
In which shades of stars're as if pearls scatter,
Th' Ri'er surface like a mirror floats in th' air.
Lights of the moon and stars make night wither ②,
Dews tide and moisten e'erything 'neath sky fair ③.

---

① **the River** the Yangtze River.

② **wither** fade away gradually.

③ **fair sky** clear sky.

暮 归

霜黄碧梧白鹤栖，
城上击柝复乌啼。
客子入门月皎皎，
谁家捣练风凄凄。
南渡桂水阙舟楫，
北归秦川多鼓鼙。
年过半百不称意，
明日看云还杖藜。

Returning to Home at Vesper

White cranes perch on Pheonix tree with frosted leaves yellow,
The night watch sounds startles crows to cry on the tower.
I enter my home gate while th' moon is shining aglow,
From whose abode th' clothes-beating sounds with wind chiller?
I crave to 'turn to Chang'an but it's caught in warfare,
And try to cross th' Guishui River but no boat to ply.
O'er fifty, I ne'er live a life to my own desire,
Let it be, morrow I'll, with stick, see the clouds in sky.

登岳阳楼

昔闻洞庭水①，

今上岳阳楼。

吴楚②东南坼，

乾坤③日夜浮。

亲朋无一字，

老病有孤舟。

戎马关山④北，

凭轩涕泗流。

---

① 洞庭水：洞庭湖，位于今湖南北部，长江南岸，系我国第二大淡水湖。

② 吴楚：春秋时二国名（吴国和楚国），其地略在今湖南、湖北、江西、安徽、江苏、浙江一带。

③ 乾坤日夜浮：日月星辰和大地昼夜都飘浮在洞庭湖上。据《水经注》卷三十八："湖水广圆五百余里，日月出没于其中。"乾坤：天地，这里指日月。

④ 关山：古称陇山，又曰陇坻、陇坂、陇首。

Ascending the Yueyang Tower ①

I've heard of th' famous Dongting Lake ② since long ago,
Now I ascend Yueyang Tower to enjoy its view.
The lake splits Wu and Chu ③ 'to th' east and south away,
The sun and moon flash in the water night and day.
From my kith and kin I have received no letter,
Wan and aged, I live with a lone boat as my partner.
On the north of Guanshan ④, many a war-steed neighs,
Leaning on the window, I shed tears down my face.

---

① **Yueyang Tower** a tower built on the city wall of Yueyang City, adjacent to the lakeside of Dongting.

② **Donting Lake** a lake located in the north of Hunan Province, the second large fresh lake in China.

③ **Wu and Chu** two states during Spring and Autumn Period, located in the present Hunan, Hubei, Jiangxi, Anhui, Jiangsu and Zhejiang.

④ **Guanshan** a mountain located in Gansu Province; also called Longsh Mountain.

南　征

春岸桃花水，
云帆枫树林。
偷生长避地，
适远更沾襟。
老病南征日，
君恩北望心。
百年歌自苦，
未见有知音。

A Southerward Journey

The spring tide brims th' banks with peaches in blooming,
My boat with cloud-white sails passes by th' maple woods.
I flee to th' place 'way from home for surviving,
In hideaway, face with tears and heart in moods.
Though wan and aged, I fare for th' southward journey,
But I still owe th' grace to th' emperor sublime.
I've not met th' one who really understand me
Though I've written poems for a whole lifetime.

江　汉

江汉思归客，
乾坤一腐儒。
片云天共远，
永夜月同孤。
落日心犹壮，
秋风病欲苏。
古来存老马，
不必取长途。

The Hanshui River

Roving in Jianghan, for my hometown I'm pining,
In th' boundless world I'm merely a scholar slight ①.
Roving in th' end of sky, I'm as if a cloud 'drifting,
And as lonely as the moon during the night.
I still aspire though aged as the sun's descent,
The autumn wind seem to drive the illness away.
An old horse ② has been ever reared since th' ancient
'Cause, 'stead of might, his wit can be called into play.

---

① **slight** unimportant, marginal.

② **old horse** a metaphor for an old man as the poet himself who dominate in wit but not in strength.

江南逢李龟年

岐王宅里寻常见，
崔九堂前几度闻。
正是江南好风景，
落花时节又逢君

Coming Across Li Guinian① in the River-South②

I used to see you show in Prince Qi's Mansion tall,
And also heard and heard you sing in Lord Cui's Hall.
The River-South's now bathed in the scenery fair,
In th' alien land we meet at the time the blooms fall.③

---

① **Li Guinian**, a Court musician during the reign of Emperor Xuanzong, and also a friend of the poet.

② **the River-South** here referring to the region covering Hunan and its adjacency.

③ **the time the blooms fall** It not only refers the real situation in which the poet came across his friend Li Guinian, but also a metaphor implying their roving life in a desolate situation, and even the declining Tang Dynasty.

过洞庭湖

蛟室围青草，
龙堆隐白沙。
护堤盘古木，
迎棹舞神鸦。
破浪南风正，
回樯畏日斜。
湖光天共远，
直欲泛仙槎。

Crossing the Donting Lake

The grass grows rank around th' Flood Dragon's Cabinet ①,
Amid the White Sand Lake looms the Gold Sand Islet.
Many ancient trees take up the Lake strands around,
The divine crows over my boat are soaring round.
Braving the due south wind, the breakers she's surfing,
I oar my boat to return when th' sun is setting.
The beauteous hue of the lake sets off the vast sky,
On th' endless lake, to sail a fairy boat I try.

---

① **the Flood Dragon's Chamber** a metaphor for the Dongting Lake.